Spells for the Wicked

by Marc Vincenz

Unlikely Books
www.UnlikelyStories.org
New Orleans, Louisiana

Unlikely Books
www.UnlikelyStories.org
New Orleans, Louisiana

Spells for the Wicked

Reality is an illusion, so why not try to express it.

The Order in Which They Appear

Dipping Toes in the Holy River

A Roman Holiday with Perky Fountains

Spells of Chivalry and Honor

Spells for the Wicked

A Rock, A Monolith, A Mountain

Bowled over,
then upended.
Lapped by water.
Carried off by
ice in a storm.
Breathed upon.

Sniffed upon.
Pissed upon.
Setting the foundations
of a new happy family.
Sandwiched between
two rusting metal poles.
Egg-scrambled here for
seventeen hundred years.
Crumbling.
Scattered.
Dug up.
Sifted.

Churned.
Collapsing.
A sandcastle.
An itinerant hermit.
A crab's home. Meanwhile,
the crab is fished, then ground
into a fine meal, mixed
with garlic,
breadcrumbs,
parsley and thyme.
Now a fine powder,
momentarily
sublime.

Eye of the Horde

Thirteen and
eight-tenths
of a billion years
in the making.

Behind the Curtains, Someone Said:

Beauty is the birth
of nothing—and, with that,

which she barely endured,
was the compass carrying

her own direction.

Imagine this, dear citizen:

the information required
to make a full movie,

is withheld by virtue
of discretion;

something apportioned

in wide-eyed increments:
information, which,

by virtue is nothing
more than beauty.

All the World's a Juicy Oyster

I know,
    I know,

        we begin
           here
in this
    realm
        of nothing-
           ness,
              which,
                in some
    might
        instill
          a sense
            of rigorous
              place- &
                stake-hold-
                ing. Bound-
              aries,
           after all,
         must be
       defined
    by land-
              marks
          viewable
       from a fair
      distance,
    or so,
the say-
ing goes:

we ap-
portion
our-
selves
in tiny,

little,
mini
incre-
ments.

A Bestiary

All the lions have gathered claiming their space
as kings and queens of beasts; the others hold

their own, stand firm in their respective fields
of expertise: those who congregate, those who scry,

those who hold back in waiting, and those who fly
above this pasture of incidental pleasures, where

across the valleys and the forested inclines,
all manner of life may be pounced upon.

Up high, the eagle stakes her claim. That one is mine!
she cries. The other birds hold back, allowing

themselves to be carried aloft by thermals,
until their majesties have had their fill.

On telephone poles, ravens and sparrows
eye the scene from all angles, working the currents

and the updrafts of pollen and bees—they know
the best meat is near the heart: firm yet malleable:

the battle for the last scrap of flesh continues.

Shoulder Roll: A Prayer

The entire corpus moves in synch
to what feels obscure, unidentifiable,

seemingly insignificant, unnecessary;
a flickering if anything at most. For all

those presumptions made, the highliving
accumulated in pounds of sugar,

or the weight of the hot sun overhead,
burning all those fertile pastures

to bread for the sake of a god-soul
who dwells in the outer atmosphere,

beyond the rain and the clouds,
beyond an entire corpus of mythologies

that wind their way down the narrow
passages of the labyrinth of the mind,

where minotaurs and other methodical
constructs move in sync with what

feels obscure, unidentifiable, seemingly
insignificant, unnecessary: a flickering.

Bread

Where civilization begins,
weeds grow.

Years of Fine Television

Behind, beyond, before light
meets her material self,

she meets her maker, at least,
so she believes as she illuminates

this late-night discussion
among cold acquaintances:

well-known gangsters and thieves
counting cards and notes.

A gun holster hangs on a nail
in the foyer patrolled

by Wolf and the Fox.
They have an eye on the sanctuary.

Back in the security guard's room,
Serpent scans the screens,

but light flickers, and shadow
and illumination blend; the cocktail

surprises where light
meets her material self,

and the citrus-hit
after the five-card stud

only adds to the contortion;
eyes are raised, but light

passes through to the other side.

Watch how matter may be destroyed
by matter! mutters the Crocodile King.

How words may become nails!
growls Rumbling Bear.

Down near the transom,
the air slurs, babbles, then,

speeds up near the fan belt,
chopped into more diffused particles,

but begins to find a firm halt.
Wolf and the the Fox pace

the halls. Still, the movie
continues with whitewashed walls—

and behind, locked in embrace,
three blind mice reach

a gentleman's agreement—
and light makes her flight along

the stairwell, through the pantry,
and oozes quietly into night.

The World Could Be Yours

The best guess
is we're incredibly
fortunate.

Tie a black thread
around your big toe
and keep on praying.

Final Spell for the First Part of the Book

So, with expatriation
the mystery might be resolved.

I hate to be the elephant in the room,
but the draft horse in me wants to walk
in straight lines, plow a path ahead.

Understandably, nothing can be verified
without clear documentation: testaments
and codices have their work to do too;

after all, who would decipher this
long after the English has been forgotten.

Understandably nothing will compliment this.

We walk the thin plowshares—wobbly, but
with a clearly delineated mythodology.

Full Speed Ahead

On a morning
like this one

billows of smoke
rise into the sky.

The factory has started
production again.

You can smell it
entwined in the oxygen.

Soon the rivers will be
running with dead fish again.

Down at your feet,
a bumblebee struggles to keep aloft;

she weaves through weeds and out
into the scrub snarled in plastics.

How to untangle
a spell twisted like this, again?

How to Build a Common Cold

Cosmic Alignment

We wander from star to star
looking for planets
in Goldilocks zones,

for meltwater and radio signals,
methane and carbon dioxide,
fragments of life shored

a trillion miles away, rushing
into existence, urgently leaving
evidence on petrified rock,

on gold or diadems,
on obelisks and menhirs,
standing stones, anything

that might pass eternal scrutiny;
but then, to transplant that find
and scatter that seed upon another

un-expecting cluster
of ur-cells who go about making
their own private business; yet,

without the misconduct
to cultivate land and sea and sky,
without the epithets to grace temples—

and, just as one might enter an oyster:
that slipping into the gullet
followed by an instant of delight,

suggesting the saline rush of oceans,
the mouthwash of moon tides—
and once again, the surge of planets

meeting their end-time
in the crush of a quasar;
or the ramifications of a tongue

upon the devilish surfaces of hot asphalt;
within the particulates of anoxic fumes—
know this: the Bull of Heaven

will return to fight the same battle
over and over, until in the end,
finally, the hero always wins.

Thieves' Canto

for Bardolph in the Bardo, where the hero always wins …

One: Catalyst

Suffer me in holy water ...

Somewhere near Daemon's Ridge,
Timeon weighs his essential salts, counts
his ducks, geese, chickens, douses himself

in the anointing oils he pilfered last night
from the Temple of Unknown Saints.

In Escallia, he spreads his essential crystals
on Dolmetsch Strasse, down Sigismund's Byway,
by way of the canal, scattering some into the water,

some on the shoes of passers by, some across
a freshly painted balustrade.

In a liminal fashion, he leaps
cobblestone to cobblestone; a hooded robe
passes uttering devotions of love

into the hedgerows; a mouse twitches,
weaves, leaps, vanishes.

Timeon too wishes to disappear into a hole
or a hedgerow—salt is scattered to save the soul;
he believes rock crystal

from the Roof of the World,
will give him his best chances in the Bardo.

Two: Consigliere

Find me an enchanted island ...

With salt on his fingers
   and dirt in his nails,
Timeon enters the derelict building:

In a former life in Byzantium,
I had three Nubian slaves,

each more beautiful than the other,
he whispers to himself
(something he is apt to do

in this age of miscommunication); and
he considers how messages are filtered

and filleted and truncated
to present whatever words
might be needed to win

a grand presidential campaign:
the grandest presidential campaign.

How they should have abhorred
the cellphone, he posits out loud, pocket-dialing
the daily password to his home security system.

Meanwhile, staring down for scraps, a rat scuttles up
a pipe and across the rotting rafters.

Timeon enters an old, dented refrigerator,
wipes the sparkles from his eyes, depresses
a colorful pad of blinking buttons behind

an oceanic array of steam ovens,
enters an elevator and descends.

In the Hitherworld, the halls
arise in incandescent light, walls higgledy-piggledy
plastered in dog-eared posters of the early Bamberg

and Hollywood starlets: *Stories once told,*
messages from the sometime-slinky, once-alive.

But the snails are all dead,
rumbles the apparition blinking
with their polyurethane eyes,

fluttering with their long nylon lashes.
The stars too are spinning into infinity, they say,

tugging on their artificial diamondstudded
earlobe, turning to face Timeon
with their deeply wrinkled silicone skin;

the narrative commences
as Timeon takes a seat and deeply sighs.

Do you think these hollowed-
out wings can lead you to-
ward your enchanted islands, Timeon?

They are made of data and light.
Just like the worlds that surround you.

From the depths of their cloud-chamber,
the apparition rises, stretches their virtual wings,
encircles the entire chamber in a cloud

of feathers and almost appears to embrace Timeon.
Come closer, my angel, they whisper in their high baritone.

You know you are my favorite child, they say.
This will be your last duty to your 1000-year-old Maw-Paw.
Timeon has heard this before, but the virtual wings surprise.

You scattered the salts, yes? Timeon nods.
That arouses me to no end, the apparition says.

Through the tips of their wings, the apparition
enters the organic mind of their offspring,
turning, turning ... toward the underworld

as the antechambers arise,
a flimsy history flashes by:

antimatter weighs less
than matter, but carries
more weight, says the apparition,

in weightlessness, we find our truer selves.
Tonight, my child, you shall die for us all.

Three: Cataract

What extinct creature would you believe ...

Jesus lands on a beach somewhere
along the coast near Caldo. The large Y birds here
are loud and aggressive, their hooked

bills scraping the sand and soil
for traces of petroleum and plastic—

a bonding agent for loosely woven nests
of briar and emmer straw. The Y birds
circle above, diving and screeching;

dragon- and mayflies rush to the rushes,
worms sink themselves deep in the earth.

Jesus throws out his nets and webs,
like a spider, he collects all he can haul,
wraps the Y hatchlings in swathes of linen

and cotton, and drives back toward his boat—
only, a storm brews dark on the horizon,

a wave of rain sweeps across the sea,
then on the beach: lizards dart for cover,
crabs dig themselves in, snails go still and wait.

Jesus and his catch reach the boat drenched.
Once inside he reminds himself to light the stove.

Waiting here for the storm to pass
would be sensible on the on hand, on the other,
the customs guard will pass here at sunset;

so, reluctantly, he starts the motor, raises
the anchor, and heads along the foaming coast.

The hatchlings are screeching, calling
for their mothers. Jesus throws them handfuls
of minnows and piperfish as he tries to navigate

precarious rocks and outcrops, and then
in a moment of indecision,

his eyes fail.

Four: Concertinas

Matter created by anti-matter ...

Thirty leagues northwest, in the port of Azul
they celebrate the birth of the Second Daughter
of the Virtuous Virgins; the Priestess sacrifices

her gray Y bird to an android on Livesensing.
The good pilgrims rejoice and release themselves

upon the waterfront, in the tavernas and the markets,
all wearing their own Y bird feathers dyed
in the flagrant colors of the equinox; and

there are even those who celebrate their planetary
alignment by donning their virtual robes.

Snakeskin approaches the crowd waving her Banners
of Glory; for she is the Second Daughter. And,
as is tradition, she is presented with fruits of the sea:

insectoids, mollusks and crustaceans, in a basket
woven from the corkscrewed hair of the ocean.

In and out of the here and now she appears
as she slowly traverses the Grand Concourse,
toward the Temple of Unknown Saints, toward

her Blood Sacrifice, toward her second life;
and the Virgins lie in wait, wailing and chanting

the most ancient tones and prayers and songs,
the pilgrims kowtow and prostrate themselves,
their long frayed robes covered in dust and time,

feet tucked beneath their hems, a journey of a lifetime,
for some, the travels have been since their birth,

along the narrow mosaic mountain paths, through deserts
and across the toxic Black Swell; some have never cut
their hair, and wear it as garlands, belts or tied

crosswise over their chests in supplication, until,
facing the Second Daughter, they will be Rebirthed.

Five: Bling

For power comes from a lifetime of deep conviction ...

In and out of their minds they flowed,
into the thoughts of the other, through
the history of the other, until they realized

they were one and the same: base pairs;
still, in that realization, they came alive.

Some might call it reincarnation, others,
by the bye: the worksheets that week
had that damp, call-and-tell me vibe. Yet,

when Timeon arrived, having died the week
earlier, all but the man on the lathe were surprised.

A resurrection, just like the little Lord Jesus,
thought the man, in his flimsy loincloth
all bloody from Roman nails, Etruscan wails.

The man himself, walking across the desert
and among his people as one of themselves.

And Timeon realized he had been reborn
in another century; a place unlike any
he had ever known or conjured into

his infernal mind, and that known devilish
mango surprise with cooling coconut sprinkles:

The apparition had been.
The apparition had been killed.
The apparition had been so kind.

The apparition had been of such keen mind.
The apparition had been us all: one and everyone.

When the body has been sanctified,
the mind finds the shortest distance
known to light; which, according to Xixamitli,

upon his flimsy pedestal of Atlantic pine,
was like casting a rubber ball into the vipers' sandpit.

Six: Somewhere in South Caldo, Tangled in the Fronds

Let them come and get me ...

The Cult of the Second Daughter was not
officially sanctioned, yet she was permitted—
even in the dankest, most rancid basements

where rats lived with fleas and fleas with flagrance;
or, to put it the way of the Supreme Leader:

she was like a cold sore that passed from lip to lip.
The valley was miles below, and seemed to spread
in all vivisections. That morning the streets were cool

and gently warming, and the pilgrims kept arriving
with their handfuls of offerings: dry rice and mangos,

wildflowers and plastic bags filled with sand
from the Igorian Sea; and sometimes, for the lucky
Priestess, who poured the forever sand to count

the eternal grains of history, the grains seemed to her
like the millet that fed her nation for centuries.

Timeon was among the worshipers that fateful morn,
in his new century. He too had washed his feet
in the Holy River, despite knowing it was contaminated

with effluents and discharges
somewhere close to its glacial birth.

Overhead the clouds darkened, and a cool breeze
swept through market square where the pilgrims
were congregated. Suddenly the trees rattled

and shuddered, Y birds took to the air—headed
toward the mountains; then the rains descended

… (A bloodhound enters the scene here.
They call him Droplet, he is a decoy for the Supreme Lizard.
He strides toward the Second Daughter, howling

in the pouring rain.) The pilgrims cheer: *Matter
created by antimatter, light created by anti-light.*

Seven: Thus Spake the Owl Priestess

Skimming the surface ...

*A*nother sacrifice; some think the handouts suffice.
A fish cheek or jowl or two will do, at least,
might ease the matter, is said;

especially when you shave them fine
and scatter them over your udon noodle soup,

when you're standing in line on the stoop,
smoking Egyptian cigarettes, staring out
upon the Caldo across the lagoon

watching the Y birds cast their early threads.
Certainly, Saint Jerome has cast in his lot.

Thus spake the Owl Priestess as the wave
engulfed the congregation gathered here
against imperial decree—later the Supreme Leader

strode across his balcony waving his arms:
The Cult of the Second Daughter is no more!

And, to the gleeful roar and cries below,
Your Supreme Leader and the high priests
of the Temple of Unknown Saints sanctify you!

The cheers returned: *And to you, Our Lord!*
In the name of the father and the daughter …

And then again, overhead the clouds darkened
and a cool breeze swept through the concourse,
and out toward the ocean, the crickets went silent,

Y birds rushed to the air, headed
toward the mountains; then the rains came.

The fish have all been sacrificed for miracles.
Well who can walk on water? says One.
Two, says, *No one except perhaps*

the Omniscient Lizard who skims
the surface looking for ghosts.

Eight: Mad Harvest

Wheat is meat and more ...

Second Daughter cast wide her net and reeled in
all her pilgrims, and found she had caught a giant iguana,
who, after a coaxing and a neck-stroking, calmly

settled in her generous arms; then nestling there,
he bristled and she called him her Past and Future,

she called him her Present Patience, and she clasped him
close to her nipple, held him beyond all the others
who wished to suckle there. On that fateful day

someone had the last word, and it wasn't She,
Second Daughter who cast her net wide.

The Priestess had a face like an owl, her brows
flowed down her nose and into your inner core,
held your gaze there like a pilgrim, like a fish

flaying and flapping, skipping across the bow, only
to yet again slip overboard and end up in the ocean.

So, yes, it was hard to meet her eyes
and her brows; still, she had been apportioned
the patience, her highbrow Patient Patience

as it was said in the Great Book, though

occasionally there would be a priestess who
would look through this like light passing through,
and she would redeem her vow among the crowd.

On those days, there was not much more to do
but hold your breath for the full length

of the sermon and look for the light:
in those old days when the apparition materialized,
hailed first as the new messiah, then as Orpheus the Second

descended into the underworld to recharge
his holy batteries: *There was a world once,*

that thrived in obsequiousness, in its own obliqueness,
and in that, or a combination thereof, Timeon found

his second breath—exhaling, yet something
obscured his vision.... We had all gone blind
in the fury of that neither particle nor wave.

Or was it more of a welling up of lost souls?
And in that light, beyond the Pillars of Hercules

or the Pindar of the Present Patience
where the illusion of time and space beget
symbols scrambling in the mind, out of need or desire,

like water arriving on a lifeless rocky planet
in an ordinary solar system in an orderly galaxy,

our thief, Timeon, wondered if henceforth
he too would almost entirely transmute into
a bolt of light a trillion and a half light years old

or if some data would hold on somewhere, clinging
on to a piece of rock for two hundred million years.

Nine: Neurotoxins

Allusions lead to illusions …

Nostradamus saw seven doves burning in the sky
in what he assumed to be Florence
but was actually the belly of a whale.

Marco Polo had alluded to it in the chronicles
of his Silk Road journeys, while recanting

his former tribal allegiances, while decanting
his preferred beverage in Mongolia.
As the clouds of dust swirl in the air,

the apparition casts their last lost, from beyond,
from repast, from The Neitherherenorthere.

They resurface ancient traces of otherworldly artifacts,
like the Gilded Sword of Amagooya, the ancient
Antiklimiteria Mechanism, or The Bulbous Roots

of the legendary Bezelhog Tree: *Lurch yourself
into the future! Hold yourself higher than ever imagined,*

*become one with your future, just as Nostradamus
prophesized: after the Fall, after the providence yet scant
of evidence, after the owl priestess, having sharpened*

*her feather-beard to a fine point, cast her iron gaze
upon those newly sanctified in salt and spirits:*

*the future, the future is revealed in the viper's sandpit.
Fear is a great motivator, says the general in his four stars,
says the Empress on her bejeweled throne casting shadows.*

Ten: Data Drawn Through Light

Artificial intelligence, artificial evidence …

Data, known in her foremost
human form as evidence,
knows how to stage a crisis

and shepherd misinformation
to her best advantage.

A refugee leaves the building.

An apparition materializes.

A word begets the audience.

Which word might you ask?
Spiritual, elemental almost,

and nothing short of divine
and ethereal in nature—ergo
intangible, yet deeply felt?

In the crowd, I atone alone.

Why This Attraction to Lunar Cycles?

Once, in
an eternity,

the universe
ends.

◆

This time
today, we

are still
ending.

Their Zen Garden

When man has colonized
the stars, and Earth
their limp wasteland,

having spent all
her sun's energy
on getting man to tan,

to build a hearth
where wood and coal and oil
scorch a path on getting man

to the stars, which,
once explored will reveal
nothing more than

what we already know:
that life is everywhere,
that every microcosm

may become organic
or inorganic matter;
even materialize as

anti-matter; and in
knowing all this, deeply,
having lived secluded

in a cave, or within
a jungle, or upon
a mountain, or tucked

into a desert waste-
land, the tidy optimist gently
tends their Zen garden.

Dipping Toes in the Holy River

Napoleon Strikes a Barebacked Bargain with the Devil
Corsica, May, 1804

A one-night stand
is all he asked for.

Artichokes, Anchovies and an Academic Eclipse
Berlin, June, 2093

I. *Must*

Fritz covets this outdoor corner table seated under Die Taube's bright blue awnings where the heft of the city finds its pterodactyl wings.

Frida delivers his usual with balsa toothpicks and a wild-yeast-fermenting orange rind. Fritz paws the news; fidgets with his frayed buttonhole, fingers the petals of his copper-loaded chrysanthemum, a gift from Mistress Hermoine Hairgolt, Director of the Von Eisenstein Institute of Herbarium and Photosynthetic Metaphors.

Somewhere inside this mind he is another, he thinks, sipping on an iced tomato smoothie warmed with celeriac jelly and lime-pickled edamame.

Fritz eavesdrops on the strolling banter, the forced cackles, the fine footwork between the cobbles, the cruel nature of hard-won decisions that seal all four fates; and he gripes and he chides; and, unlike his anarchic cousins fighting on the frontline, stirs his magnetic spoon methodically, mechanically counterclockwise.

II. *Become*

Shadows stretch into the latter half of a cloudy day and swoon into misty twilight.

For a quantum minute, Fritz compiles his headlines, but then, *bisserl na bisserl*, tosses icy glances, rolls his thyroid eyes, and, from time to time, raises his left brow, then, meagerly, salutes a passing pink joyride: a nymph on her bike with honeysuckle and thyme trailing behind....

Then later, he punches his inflections, his longings and keynotes, into a padlocked diary, and the slow creep of his own bougainvillea crosses the dove shit splattered rooftops of Die Taube; amid this roaring metropolis, the four concertinas tinkle in the high hopes that in one concerted afternoon of great expectations, Fritz may discover his own alchemical enlightenment....

Yet, each day appears as the one before; and when he orders his evening aperitif and cheese plate with seeded mustard and gherkin fans, no matter the whether of pumpernickel or farm-seeded sourdough, even the most authentic antique in the city can't hide from the penumbra.

Peace, he sings, crunching on a pickle, *has been eclipsed.*

Ostrogothic

In this bearded Frankish wave
of half-commotion-half-surprise,

the Celts raise their alms high;
that each deserving god, might,

if momentarily in delight, find
the Romans and Egyptians delightfully embalmed—

tacit in their Tacitus, but surely always Epicurious;
and how much does the heart weigh

on a scale from here to nonesuch,
along the way to their dark netherworld;

or the ramblings of another unsuspected creature,
golden in locks, but dead in the bones?

Elias' answer was next to none; he stared them
head on, then turned to the unsuspecting camera,

where there are *those who see and those who hear*—
and yet, in many of these dumb-founded

technicians in all their non-seeing-and-hearing,
they lifted the hotdog in the room to a non-plus.

May we find a common pause? Was the question asked
across the candlelit, labyrinthine hedgerows.

A little zesty mustard will brighten any dish!
Elias said, eating his sausage with relish.

Stars Sailing Over Ethiopia

Only recently has it been discovered that when you recycle your truths tenfold, twentyfold; or in exoneration (all vindication erased), a thousand, the world crumbles—each of our folkloric treasures reveal themselves, as has recently been reaffirmed by Abel, an Ethiopian farmer plowing dry ruts in his soil—each and every shard of hard-boiled evidence (from the leather scabbard to the fine-toothed ivory comb engraved in lions, the spinning jenny and the hand-painted jugs, beakers and jars), demonstrate our ancestors are within reach, just beneath the upper layer.

All the evidence points to the thousands who have made their intrepid journeys into the heart of a smooth continent, over arid hinterlands, or into the crude heart of civilization to find religion, magick, or to seek spiritual guidance to align themselves with star formations, constellations, or the ACTGs of the deep quantum soup (those double-stranded base pairs in their fractal loop).

And, no, we won't go romantic and mythologize all those trillions of suns; we shall simply stand here at night and imagine that some day all this will finally be over.

Mountain River Cave

Idyllic in her presentation, and
waiting for the tenderest word.

So much freedom is bewildering,
she thinks, wavering in her splendor,
and wonders if she has ventured
that much closer to the gods; later, she stirs
the brook waters with her fingers,
looking for faint wisps of life;
instead she feels the pulse
burning in her wrist.

Her circulating blood is proof
that these liquids and their deep infinities,
make her want to explode
into a billion fragments,
that she might finally sleep
like a dying sun.

Gastric Bypass

She sips her tiny cervesa and chews her teeny tapa:
a mini black olive marinated in lemon and rosemary
skewered on a frilly cocktail-stick; she takes her petite nibbles
and contemplates the meaning of her long second marriage.

Thirty chews for a morsel no larger than her little fingernail.
Besides, she says, they muck up her new braces.
She's thinner than I last saw her, but not too much,
she's been indulging since her last cockatoo, Captain Redbird,

died from the lead paint he stripped off his bamboo perch
with the Captain Morgan logo and the *Aye Aye Capt'n.*
Those Chinese factories will do anything for a greenback, she says fingering
her hot bleached hair, raising her Yves Saint Laurent

sunglasses and pursing her lips into a frothy epithet:
Pet stores are in cahoots. Chinese are driving up cat food prices.
She says, when recently she tried to squeeze into her old bikini,
her husband guffawed at the love handles that formed

along her hips and the cellulite on her upper thighs.
Who wants to tumble and roll with a fatty, she says, taking out her
compact and reapplying her grey-blue eyes.
For months she resorted to eating parrot food:

hard, seeded biscuits that tasted like crunchy grains
of bitter coffee, a business in which, by the way, her love-bundle,
Ivor, was a big investor; he had plantations
as far afield as Indonesia, and money was no issue,

so he had her stomach stapled to half its burgeoning size.
Now a single raisin is a full meal, which is delightful when Ivor
wants to slide her in beside him like a sleek slip of crisp paper.
The little her inside, says she, remains persistently beautiful.

Glasnost

This time of year
it all shifts, slips,
scuttles ahead—

perhaps un-
appreciative
of the subtle

nature of sensory
perception,
bursts of radiation

cascade across
the mountains,
down into the valleys

where deer and ibex
graze the pastures
and rocky outcrops—

Everything is trans-
parent, the grasses
whisper softly;

meanwhile, the man
with the nightstick
prods you gently

in the chest,
asking politely
for your trans-

it papers.

Three Moths and a Nymph in a Bucket of Fiery Piss

In ancient Rome, buckets of piss
frothed and sloshed on every corner,
and those wry mystics, passing
and imbibing that sulfuric aroma,

touched the muddy hemlines
of perpetually leaking gods, who too
had pissed down Cobblestone Lane
into the latrine and along the laundry line;

and bear in mind, back then there were no
laundromats or dry-cleaners;
garments were plunged into the fiery piss
collected at crossroads, turned and spun

and whirled with giant wooden ladles
until they had become enamored
with the human genome and decided
to spill their guts down into antediluvian sewers

where those effluents wandered, until,
they reached out into the undying ocean
where the twelve-headed Hydra collected
her wealth of senators' and emperors'

incontinence; and, even as her hand
reached out to blow back that kiss,
Herculaneum lay in Vesuvius' lava and ash,
its citizens embalmed in molten rock.

A Seat at the Bar of Non-Being

I favor those
public displays
where they scatter

like roaches
in their search
for prime ingredients

to make their very best
version of history
(perhaps with

a little chopped
humility and buttersautéed
elephant

memory, or shaved
freeze-dried
flakes of Arctic char

cheek, doused
in a century of history,
cask-aged Sanlúcar

de Barrameda,
that reaches out
to grasp a little

Ostrogothic wisdom:
solar flares
guide the way

through the finest
Icelandic sunstone;
and when served up,

doused and slowroasted
in Etruscan
olive oil

with shavings
of ripened
constitutional cheese,

or wrapped
in iridescence;
a conscious foliage

born of primeval seas,
as indeed,
in Chiang Mai,

in their vibrant
shoe soles and
deeply ingestible

greenery); either
way, they hurtle
through striking

insolent poses,
waving and saluting
for the autofocus

as they search
their pockets
loudly, fitfully,

for prime ingredients
to make their very best
version of history.

A Myth Like No Other

I. *Outwardly Bounded*

Specters circumnavigate the metropolis,
farmers circle towering dynasties
in their oily formations, industrialists cower
in fetal positions determining which course
to flow after the fever has subsided.

The meager potentiate claim to know her
from her nighttime bruises, the light-brown
dapple of her near-fatal furless skin.

And then, they hone in, knowing
at this mortal's feet everything
has been appeased, yet still, the aphrodisiac
consumes the growing populace.

101 days pass thus, onward, within-without.
Not chained to a rock, but dragging Mother Earth
at her heels. Still, Eve moves one toe ahead of another,
hem to foot to hem to surface; all potentialities
driving forward on a linear sublime; or so she thinks.

Eventually, one third of a sprightly year drifts by.

Toward the end of those days, even the rain thinks
she's straightening out matter: creeks and rivers
overflow, roads crack and split and shed; and,
eventually, matter, once again, rises to the surface—
and she's bubbling in felicity within all that surface tension:

There are satyrs who wait, and those who point.
We'd hoped she'd be one of the latter.

II. *On a Day Like This*

Day 102, and, as a raven she caws:
A god should be able to frighten a person
to death, and then, easily revive them....
And still, she hovers over her wife's insolent corpse
as if she were the keystone to his new city;

and she shakes her to revive her, and she roars to the gods;
but eventually, declares in her honor, from whence
new generations of philosopher-gods should arise:
the Temple of Immaculate Being. Later, she asks
if she should fall upon her sword like an emperor

lost in campaign, or if something else might appease
the universe and her all-consuming blood-thirst.
And yet, in time, or in the passing of it, the tenuous unsanctified
warrior, emboldened by a sweet lilac scent
that reminds her of a vertiginous youth

on the sacred Isle of Syringia, bounds upon those volcanic pastures
as if hell-spurned on reviving some older part
of her younger soul. The cards have prophesized; the fingers
do the bitter turning; the vipers' tongues, the fast talking.
And wouldn't you have liked to see a duck egg or two

tossed forth in this overburdened cloudless work;
and sadly not, sadly not, no one quite matches
the descriptions, and quite recently, they flew south.

But where is the abyss in all that? she says.

An idea of perfection persists.

III. *By Any Other Hand*

Idle conversation and lesser action
are less bitter than the last leaves of smoke,
says she to herself; and, wonders of the inaction
of watchmen shadowing
watchers in their wake, themselves.

Perhaps we shall never know what occurred
that 102nd night, beneath the cover
of faint moonlight, when she walked back
to the surface of the earth, but then, in amongst
the clumps of dirt and weeds, the serpents arose,

their jagged tongues licking the surface
of the mellow-blue sky and they whispered
that someday someone should discover
the Simulacrum, a device that once served
the common people, buried three feet deep,

beneath arms and fingers and skulls, reaching out
as flesh and bone, in their darkest intentions.
When the half-naked empress encircled
her mother's fortunes, she said to her retinue:
Are there no lions performing among you anymore?

A single courtier raised their hand high above:
Your Divine Grace, I would gladly roar for you!

The high tricks of burden prove burdensome.

Who doesn't want to be cast into space
and become a sheer constellation?

Unholy Alliance

The head of a religious state
stares at you during dinner,

wipes his lips with the corner
of his polyester napkin, winks,

twitches, takes a slow cat-lapping slurp
of his cabernet; lays his golden wrists

on cheap white tablecloth, almost
in supplication, but more in injunction;

turns his pale palms toward the ceiling:
up there is nothing but the Malthusean

dome holding up urban planning;
and then, turning to the audience,

straightens his eyebrows, clears
his impetuous throat, and says:

We are ants, ladies and gentlemen,
we collect sugars to power the hive,

to feed the young and infirm,
to inform the generations to come.

Once I was a beekeeper, and I believed
the beehive was the crowning glory

of an organized society....

You can see them all
crawling over his back.

All the Common Folk

Are wearing
condoms

according to
imperial decree;

which means,
of course, folk

are measuring
themselves up....

In the Abode of Felicity

Where the means
of happiness thrives,

where you are assumed to be
contented and your skin

is firm like a fish,
your belly shaped like a quince.

The emperor decides all this
in his fruity abode, shaped like a peach

(he loves that velvety bounce,
like moss on rotting wood)

while putting golf balls
into cosmic toilet bowls

or playing tiddlywinks
with well-dressed courtiers.

Every standard is proscribed
and prescribed in a multinational

ledger that floats like a storm cloud
hovering over the iCloud:

rain on top of rain,
and all that life within, stirring.

It Must Have Been Something She Ate

If a man believes he is going to die, he'll die a lot quicker than if he doesn't.

It was a bad morning,
and an even worse
afternoon spent on the bench,

awestruck with the bacilli
that had transferred
lipid to lip, tongue to tit.

Sometimes they would settle
on her nether regions
and home in on the urine buzz;

that something recycled by human filters
that shines through the fabric
of her essential waters;

and by then, they would drift there,
drawn in by the furious intensity,
and they would be reminded

of their own origins,
the slime and muck
of previous generations,

and the dragonflies skimming
over thick green algae, filling
their heads with all sorts of chlorophyll.

The Wasp Factory

Father's cigar
smoke always

knew best,
and infused

our balustrades,
and banisters

with a little hint
of young Fidel.

Meanwhile,
all the spooks

pointed north,
at least those

who had been
magnetized

by the wasp
queen's iron sting.

A Very Obscure Diagnosis

On an even Sunday
the daemons appear
at the courthouse.

They're demonstrating
a movie—something like that;
I've been told it involves a black cat.

They wave their magic antlers
to the tune of *God Save Our Souls,*
and it has us truly befuddled.

Apparently, the lead actor
(they're called Wednesday or Friday;
either way, an uneven day of the week),

appears at the opening as a twelve-pointed
daemon known to frequent alleys
with a cat named Heliotrope.

"Who doesn't have daemons
in their basement," Pa Rat says innocently
staring at the gelatin dribbling down the panes.

"Is that all you see out
the window?" his wife says
pouring the eternal milky tea.

A Roman Holiday with Perky Fountains

Once Upon a Time in Liechtenstein

I.

Raycheff doused his garden fitfully.
With all his wells and watering holes

springing up his side of the partition,
he imagined having exclusive

rights to the water supply
of the Prince of Liechtenstein

and his lunchtime crew of demagogues.
Still, as Raycheff's sunflowers

and petunias opened their minds,
with their own bees and mayflies,

they stared him head on, encouraging,
nay insisting; and, in the meantime,

attempting to impart a little
of their own honeyed wisdom.

They said: *From which cultural
wellspring did you emerge, Sister?*

They said: *You know the desire for sweetness
is deeply embedded, Brother.*

II.

And in that instant, Raycheff realized he needed the water
for his own nursery; and he swore to all his ancient gods,

he would build an immaculate garden,
an arboretum like no other on his side of the planet:

more beautiful than Versailles,
more sublime than Giverny,

more all-encompassing than Kew Gardens.
His sunflowers would be

the proud purveyors of a discreet
insight, something from the bosom

of Aphrodite herself; and thus,
Raycheff trussed himself

in the trappings of the Golem,
the costume of which, now lying

decrepit in its own grave of hell-bent
moss, is *lichening up*. Raycheff set

to his powers of design, and stretching
his imagination in impropriate ways convulsed

upon a formula of dramatic proportions,
himself, precluded; but, having trenched in,

received such gentle proportion
and propulsion, he bent in upon himself,

and removed his organs one by one;
donating each of them for a specific purpose:

the heart for the roses, eyes for the sunflowers,
kidneys for the lilacs and lilies, bladder

for the chrysanthemums; pancreas for poppies;
and as he embedded each of his vitals

within the topsoil he slowly became one
and the water flowed and sputtered

and slowed and sputtered and babbled
and rippled and sputtered and drizzled.

III.

Raycheff knew:
the telltale signs.

Old age had taught him well.

IV.

He felt his intensity fading and dwindling,
until eventually he coughed fitfully,

then, in a single enigmatic sigh....

Purge of the Apparition *(An Epilogue of Sorts)*

Spectacles

Back in those days
we had no spectacles.

We used magnifying glasses
and shards of broken crystal

you could find on the banks
of the Holy River;

as children we scoured
the pyres and ashes, and

scattered here and there,
sometimes found grief,

gold teeth and earrings.

Folks who had the holy eye
were much called upon.

Visions

Julia was one of those,
and she dispensed her visions

along the muddy shores
for pilgrims seeking passageway

for their deceased mothers,
for their distant fathers,

husbands, dislocated wives
into the Hitherworld;

as she plied her trade,
she was alone among us

yet still one of our kind.

Folks who had the holy eye
were much called upon.

Smoke

When Julia cast her eyes
upon the fires and the smoke,

she could see spirits rising
and falling—the blue flame,

she said, was the origin of us all,
and within that flickering,

the very essence of the self
was to be found. In 2254,

they would crack the code.

It was then the apparition
made their appearance.

They said, *Time is irrelevant:*
4 billion years, twenty thousand?

Exalted

We said, Who are you
to tell us where there's smoke

or where there's light?
We said, Find your definition.

Whatever it takes, from the origin.
And within that flickering,

we hunkered down, deep
in the vault, where seeds

had been saved from an apocryphal
flood, born on the Tiber, Indus or Nile.

It was then the apparition
made their appearance.

They said, *Time is irrelevant:*
4 billion years, twenty thousand?

Nothing

300,000 years in context.

In the 200,000,000,000 galaxies
in the observable universe

is there no intelligence?

Shadow God

She arrives in the city
dirty and disheveled
from her long trek
through backcountry

but holds herself high
like a tree or a rose,
and eventually the city
comes to her with open palms,

pats on the back or the backside
with wide-eyed smiles
and an intoxicated cheer, as if
always expecting her to roll in

on a wave of crude innocence;
yet, unbeknownst to them,
she has them by the drawstrings,
nimble fingers

plying them as marionettes,
or the bamboo pickup sticks
of the *Nan Talung*—shadows
against backlit rice-thin paper....

Yes, she has considered nearly
everything, all the way down
to the mitochondrial. You need
to sacrifice for success, she says,

eyeballing the glass fisheye
that travels up her cheongsam,
over her boundless curves
and hollows, speckled plains

and meadows of moist skin,
all the way along her shoulder
and neck, briefly scanning
the half-moon mole on her chin,

the purse of her lips—
her seaweed-green hair,
glistening, enchants, awakens
an ocean within:

and thus the tide returns
to the city, through her dense
considerations, through her dark
always, through her satisfied purr.

Al Zahara

A collection of emptiness
scattered across three million square miles
all hoping for torrential rain;

offerings on the grave of someone
who despised religion, who
in the frenzied expanses of megacities,

for the greater good, endured
the quest for the answer to every question:
to control nature is its great autonomy.

Cross the wastelands and you will see
there is much more here than believed;
of course, Al Zahara, herself endures,

sanctifies, cleanses the essence of all impurities,
leaving the soul empty to be seeded
with the divine word once again.

The blind seer tells me this has all
been seen and heard before: each and every grain,
a thought or an impulse, each dune

a civilization moving toward
her next incarnation. When the young
try and reclaim Al Zahara—hearts

thudding against the stillness—
they are struck with awe.
You cannot reclaim all those thoughts,

say their old mothers and grandmothers.
Think of it another way, say their uncles.
Fathers and grandfathers too, chime in:

A collection of madness is what this is!
Meanwhile, a new religion is discovered
stirring beneath the desert sands.

Things That Dangle Themselves in Your Head

Anchovies. Seaweed. Conger eels. Carrots. Paper cuts.
Origami knots. An open hand. An open sewer. Oily beards.
Fringes. Angioplasty. Salubrious objections. Cold mint tea.

Swagger. Cricket and crickets. *Fledermäuse*. Snickers® bars.
Snippets. Gyrating hips. Hot toffee apples. Snapple®.
Stuffed chili peppers. Ink blots. Mountain goats. Muppets®.

A tight fist. Punch and Judy Show. Roasted almonds.
Vacant lots. Geothermal subterranean vents. Crushed beer cans.
Graffiti. Escalators. Garlic, garlic, garlic. Fish sauce. Black Roses.

Violins. Vampyres in the lemongrass. Snakes in the woods.

Twisted spirits. Twisted spines. Fingers twisted in the curry.
Diamond earrings. Butter croissants. Dark chocolate.
Diamond mines. Midas touch. *Moctezuma*. El Dorado.

Jaipur, Dar es Salaam, Lagos. Soiled fingernails. Thyroids.
Larynxes. Scabs. Quinces. Minces. Jellied sardines. Platypuses.
Jelly-fish. Fishy cloud-work wafting away. Crustaceans. Whales.

Fingerspitzengefühl. Mettre la main à la pate. Goose-step finger-walking.
Crispy fish sticks. Goose liver pate. Grass skirts. Bamboo puppets.
Panda bears and firebreathers. Adobe vats and jars. Raisins,

Raisinets®. Raisin Bran®. Chloroform. Patent pending.
OxyContin®. Scratched Teflon®. Mercury. Radiation poisoning.
Thumbs up. Thumbs down. Smiley face. All thumbs.

Spell for the Middle of the Road

Never cross a chicken.

Before Farms Were Run by Artificial Intelligence

I.

Nobody is looking ahead, but seized
yet stirring in a political tide,
and, the wave of probabilities still persists.

Perhaps there is an element of laziness,
a warm subterfuge to benignly smile
under the eye of the landowner-beholder.

How much love is needed to build
a combine harvester? To wake the sleeping
farmers from their downy pillows?

With barley and durum and flax
and emmer; with corn and soya
and rice; with potato and plantain,

and cocoa and coffee, with tea
and tomatoes and transnational milk;
with pasteurized and hydrogenated citizenry,

sodium nitrate and her half brother, monosodium
glutamate will find their pathways
in to all their arteries, and the sugars

will coalesce on their shores; and the question
posed was: where is all the energy spent and assigned?
And then, how and when is it apportioned out?

II.

Is it a matter of faith that these creatures
will, as a matter of course (or DNA, if you will),
will themselves into the concept of efficacy

in ultimate, perhaps celestial design,
that life is self-fulfilling, ever-adaptable,
continuously evolving toward the future;

and therefore the faith suggests that the creative
principle, tendency, inclination—that trial-and-
error, learning-by-doing, slow accumulation

has led us to this very point in history, the moment
the landowner-beholder reads us our due diligence.
If not we, who would take charge? they chant.

A Crow Delivers Salient Points

It becomes easier to search for worms
when you're at ease with the breeze.

Bones with traces of marrow
are to be found everywhere.

Follow the sound of the largest beak—
they will know how to peck and sing.

Tear flesh as close to the sinew
as your reach may allow.

Follow the wolves.
Follow the lions.

Use your shadow to create panic,
then, perch and wait.

Don't show off your plumage unless
you're absolutely sure yours is brightest.

Allow the magpie and the jackdaw
their little misgivings.

Give off no known odor by rubbing
yourself in a cocktail of slime and mud.

Learn to observe everything
from far far above.

Comment only when called upon.
Comment sporadically or just nod your head.

Spells of Chivalry and Honor

Into the Hands of a Holy Roman Citizen

Seventeen denarii from a Sicilianus
Twelve talents from a bald, yet hairy Ostrogoth.
Nine silvers from Imperial Tokin.
Three bronze pelts from the Antilokos
in exchange for an ivory tusk and a tiny red ruby.

I too was acquired by the Roman Empire,
where once, in the center of the Coliseum
my *Ladin* ancestor stood, trident and net in hand
facing the crocodiles on one side, the lions
on the other; meanwhile a barbarian queen

approached at full tilt, her chariot tearing
through the sand as if she had been a stuntdouble
in Charlton Heston's *Ben Hur*, or,
perhaps my ancestor had been a parsimonious git:
a wheeler-dealer just like my immediate *pater familias*;

who, when in a corner, would inevitably pull out
his dice, and toss, and toss, and toss, until
the numbers added up. You could count
on him to go for the sweet deal, but build
a little buffer on his side; and then, when through,

the world became his own very oyster—even though
he loathed them: *far too oceanic for my alpine tongue*—
and he tongued and nibbled and lip-synced,
his mouth full of perfunctory notes, in exchange
for a mouthful of compote and a lap-dance:

anything for the wife and kids back home.
And across the planet he soared in search
of profits, polecats and polemic, ending up
in bars and restaurants on the edge of the known:
in the jungles of Indonesia, the turquoise shores

of Pacific islands, the white sandy beaches
of polyamorous nation-states. They say,
on his wedding night, he left the conjugal bed
and wound his way through the streets of Tokyo,
shored into a Yakusa dive, the ShinJuku Wave,

where Kirosaku was waiting with three
Osakan pearl divers, stripped to the waist
and ready to submerge into their element.
Angie wound her way through the wet streets
of Tokyo, and found him, two of the sprites

sitting on his lap and feeding him peanuts.
She slapped him around the head, tore the martini
from his hand and downed it, three olives and all
(or maybe they were pickled onions); still,
he laughed on, teasing the knees of Yuko.

Aiko, on the other hand, reached behind the bar
and pulled out an ancient German Luger, loaded
and ready at the hilt. *We're gonna take you!* she said,
and true to her word, shot what appeared to be
lukewarm sake straight in Angie's tired face.

A Polynesian bouncer, by the name of Tahito
appeared behind the curtain flexing his tattoos
and ordered our *pater* to pay up or get out,
and thus he did, staggering home in the rain
propped under Angie's angry umbrella.

Like any Roman citizen in a bind, he professed
his fealty to his young wife, and swore
this was just a momentary lapse of his senses:
marriage, after all, was no laughing matter, but
Angie's silence had the last word in the Tokyo twilight.

Rome, of course, was not built in a day or two,
but grew into all its tentacular proportions
with cold steel, clear-headed military precision,
and millions of feet, hands and mouths, all
prodded in the direction of Agrippa's Pantheon.

Had he lived in the era of Hadrian, *pater noster*
should most certainly have been a fish sauce trader,
crossing the Mediterranean a hundred times or more
in his search for the fishiest business partners
even miles from the coast; it is known

family lore that our ménage was descended
from a long line of Etruscans or Phoenicians, who,
unhappy with their Roman usurpers, headed
upwind, into the mountains to put distance
between them and Rome; and, having settled

here, far from the madding yelp, they farmed goats,
sorrel and blueberries, yodeling on their own gumdrop
of alpine heaven; perfecting, believe it or not,
the art too of cheese, curds and whey, churning
a tidy profit for the displaced mountainfolk;

until, centuries later, they become the biggest
goat-cheese makers in *Raetia Prima*, and are thus,
once again, offered full Roman citizenship—
villas overlooking lush green valleys rose up in the Alps;
steam baths steamed, toilets had dolphin armrests

and pine-oiled apple-wood seats; a panoply of gods
cast their golden eyes upon the coniferous trees,
the mules, donkeys and oxen headed to market,
the early pâtissiers, and the well-oiled bordellos
that lined the colonnade of paved mountain avenues.

As a full Roman Citizen, *pater noster* was afforded
all rights and as result could never be crucified,
even though he strode through the killing fields
of the southern plains. All he wished to do was stand
head-high in the forum and proclaim his holy lineage.

And yet, far into the centuries, crossing the equator
a hundred times our *pater* (who art in heaven),
hallowed be his own name in deeds and misdeeds—
struck deals with men of low morals, who reaped
and raped their lands, all for the glory of Empire—

and, of course, later on, honeymoon in Hawaii
at a luau, I was inserted into this fine fecund universe—
all of Tokyo's sins forgiven, and in a vision,
the new world appeared to our *pater noster*
(it has been said it took seventeen martinis

and even more Cuban cigars—and in the end,
gladiator he claimed he was, remained the last man standing).
In his dream, a mangy lion pounced upon him
and tore his face and body into thin strands,
a herd of stampeding elephants finished him off.

The dream, he surmised was one of Hannibal
crossing the Alps to erase the once-glory of Rome.
And yes, a foreign devil dwelled in the rafters
of his own windy attic: I am much more than this,
he sometimes said when drunk or tired or dead.

In his sepulcher, his second wife, Pixie, an Ostrogoth,
placed his ashes within a plastic heart. I remember her
gently caressing the surface, in which was engraved:
  In the end, as is the fate of all Romans,
  looking back, we turn to stone.

Genome

When
the I

is sur-
mised

but not
nece-

ssarily in-
ferred;

when
the I

is in-
ferred,

but not
nece-

ssarily
trans-

mogrif-
ied.

One-Hit Wonder

John and Paul set about charming
the world with their dulcet tones.

They wore their mutually thick hair
combed to the left with a side-part
just above the coronal suture.

One was jolly, the other depressed,
one was talented, the other departed;

yet, they stitched the world together;
in the very least, in their own minds,
just beneath the coronal suture.

They displayed their virtues in bars
and dives all along the eastern seaboard;
in one, Lulu's Hungry Goose, John

met his second wife, Xenia. On their wedding
night, just before their commingling,

Paul burst into the room coming apart
at the seams: he had written it, it arrived
from on a shooting star in the moonlight.

Eureka! he yelped, jumped on the bed
right between naked John and Xenia,

they giggled and started to hum Paul's song;
he called it "Mother's Song," which John felt
wasn't quite with the flow of the times, Xenia too

with her holy virtue, jumped in, her hair
cascading, her bosom uplifted, reached deep

within her inner core, sensing that this was
a seminal moment of soul-seeking;
they sang the song over and over

all through the night and into the morning.
It was when, at six a.m., John leapt up

and roared, *This is not the salt lick!*
and that decided the fate
of everything else to come.

The Citizenry

Pulverized.

Reconstituted.

Dehydrated.

Pre-packed.

Flash-frozen.

Sterilized.

Poly-unsaturated.

Colorized.

Tenderized.

Liquefied.

Acidified.

Decalcified.

Decaffeinated.

Decontaminated.

Federally amalgamated.

The Disgruntled Mythologist

In cumulus clouds above
the Pillars of Hercules,

Zeus scratches his beard,
and fleas tumble down

through the ether, landing
on Mount Olympus.

Today, the gods still dispute
which of these fleas became

the bubonic plague, and which
the human race.

A Casual Curry Party and the Glass Eye

Curries come about quite naturally;
at least, so said my old friend Kumar
while stoking his magic carpet.

Immigrants land here from all over, he said,
chewing on betel nut, pouring me
a glass of mint tea. His hands weren't steady,

so he spilled a few drops. His Amma
yelped from the kitchen (she was massaging
some kind of dough with roasted cumin):

Did you soil our magic carpet, son?

We spent hours between lunch and teatime
cleaning, then brushing said magic carpet;
honestly, to me she seemed fairly

run-of-the-Grand Bazaar. She had moth holes,
and cigar ash or hookah or cigarettes
had singed the fringes on her westerly end;

still she glowed on, her yarn count of over
100 stitches per inch, shimmering
in all our vigorous vicinities.

The curry will be ready at half past six, said Amma.

The lime pickle had been fermenting
for seven months; Amma spooned out dal
and fluffy saffron basmati, palak paneer

with leafy greens from her garden,
and goat cheese milked and cured with love
in a dilapidated barrel in her barnyard.

The owls glared in the windows as we ate,
the brazier flames rose and wavered,
the bats started circling at half past seven;

And the curry, herself, is one of oysters and clams, said Amma;

But also, fresh basil, green cherrystone chilies,
mustard seed and turmeric and ground cumin, all brought
from over the enchanted mountain on a donkey.

Halfway through dinner, the carpet quivered.
At first we thought it was a dump truck passing outside.
Kumar giggle-hiccupped, sucking on a clamshell.

And somehow, resonating with the mood,
and Amma's warm curry that rested in our bellies,
the carpet hummed an ancient tune of sheer delight.

Later that night we danced in fourteen discos, said Kumar,

and imbibed more combustible snakebite than is legally permitted.
Staggering out of Josephina's All-Night Flop Shop,
we were arrested by the fashion police.

Kumar's lungi, a cross between a short toga
and a gun holster, caught the suspecting agent's glance.
Pretending to be someone else, eh? said the cop, rolling up

to Kumar's staggering bounce, leaning against
a charred wall and staring deep into Kumar's left
eye. They stared like that for minutes.

But little did the cop know my left eye, said Kumar,

was glass; so Constable Pesh stared on,
hoping to break the eye and crack the silence
with his own steely glance. It didn't work.

Kumar's left eye stared ahead
as if he was in some kind of inside joke.
Meanwhile, his breath smelled of garlic and turmeric.

And I was convulsively burp-hiccupping, said Kumar.

Follow me at a distance, said Constable Pesh
with eyes in the back of his head.
The two men vanished down an alley

strewn with dumpsters and trash;
there was a kerfuffle, an incident,
but, by the time I reached the offending alley,

the smoke had dispersed to reveal
a single glass eye gently rocking
on the asphalt, starting straight toward me,

It was as if the universe had collapsed in that eye.

And indeed, it had: if you looked closely
you could see galaxies swirling and forming,
black holes consuming, quasars imploding;

and later, at home, when I put the eye
under a microscope, I could see Kumar
floating freely in the cosmic waters—

flying really—as if upon a magic carpet.
Years later, I stopped in to see Amma
with a bunch of wildflowers and a handful of saffron.

Even Kumar didn't know his own left eye, she said.

And she poured the mint tea, and didn't spill a single drop.

Cousteau's Calypso

Just follow the dolphins!

V is for Vulcan, Vincenz and Vesuvius

My old man praised himself for not being
like his own Pa, Old Pa, but striking out
to the furthest shores from his home:
a mildly coniferous alpine village sautéed

in pristine sunlight and chanterelle mushrooms,
where the jangle of the cowbells foretell
snowstorms, and the ghosts of Huns and Romans
walk the forest in the bewitching hours.

At the age of nineteen, he made off to the city
and sold exclusive ladies' shoes door to door.
He would barrel down the slick cobbled alleys
of Zürich's *Altstadt*, suitcase of slip-ons in each hand,

stopping off at the Schweizerhof for a cool,
frothy brew and Bratwurst with a roll and mustard,
before hitting the Bahnhofstrasse in a mildly-inebriated
vim and a more mature, youthful vigor.

His first client that day was a Mistress Nicolette Chantalle,
the bedazzling owner of La Grande Boutique Bijou,
who fussed over his Steve McQueen hairdo
and that Marilyn mole on the edge of his lip.

She purchased twenty pairs of the *Musicienne Toscano*,
a stiletto built like a tap shoe that snapped
as you trod the sidewalks. The champagne cream pair
had often featured at weddings and funerals

that previous season; this new model, however,
also possessed a Venetian buckle
made of gilded blue, blown glass from
the enchanted island of Murano.

Mistress Nicolette Chantalle invited Pa
to join her in a snifter of Armagnac and an amusebouche
of pickles with *saucisson sec*. One thing
led to another—eventually in the Liederstube,

over Crystal Brut, they danced: he, sniffing
her equine neck, she, wandering over
his long elephantine earlobes
with the tip of her delicate ivory nose.

At three o'clock in the morning, he'd slipped off
her negligee and she arched back like a panther in heat.
In that moment, between confessions
and further libations, Pa's own Pa, Old Pa,

appeared in the doorway, his back hair glimmering
in the moonlight from all the Brylcreem.
(I've been told Pa was licking Mistress Nicolette Chantalle's
engorged nipple and her left leg was raised

with her Mexican-pink toenails pointing toward
the Sistine-chapel-shaped ceiling.)
Old Pa lifts the studio couch above his head
(they said he could bench-press five fullygrown

men on an old oak door), and tosses it
in the direction of the unsuspecting couple coupling.
From that day, my old man swore
he would only ever sell industrial: factories, conglomerates,

cooperatives, wiley companies feasting on the fringes—
all run by men, vulcanized in their steadfast tread.
He held his couch-scar in high esteem,
and fondly recalled Mistress Nicolette Chantalle,

his entire lifespan, until, indeed, at the end,
he announced his undying love for her—
she, a married woman with seven children,
who, had not my mother been, would have been

his femme fatale until the end of time;
and yet, when she, Mistress Nicolette Chantalle
herself died, that bruise on her eyelid never
quite fully healed, she called out his name:

Vincenz!! she wailed, wrapping herself
in her finest Egyptian linens:
Let us resurrect together and vulcanize
in the winds of time like Vesuvius!

Spell for the Replicator

How does
one duplicate

let alone
multiply?

Looking back
into the mirror

of time,
the funda-

mental principle
evades herself.

Acknowledgments

"A Bestiary," translated by Paul Burcia into Romanian as "Bestiar," appeared in the Romanian cultural journal *TOMIS*.

"Before Farms Were Run by Artificial Intelligence" was originally published in *New American Writing 42*.

"Al Zahara" originally appeared in the *Santa Clara Review*.

"A Crow Delivers Salient Points," "A Very Obscure Diagnosis," and "Three Moths and a Nymph in a Bucket of Fiery Piss" were originally published in the *Fortnightly Review*.

"Glasnost" was originally published in the *Tourniquet Review*.

"V is for Vulcan, Vincenz and Vesuvius," appeared in *Plume*.

"Bread," "Cosmic Alignment," and "Full Speed Ahead," appeared in *Unlikely Stories*.

"Thieves' Canto," was originally published as a chapbook by Nixes Mate, Allston, Massachusetts.

Notes

"A Rock," is for Signurs Lorenz Vincenz Sr. and Jr. on the other side, who didn't believe in seafood, and hardly believed in stone.

"Cosmic Alignment," is for Joseph Campbell embedded in the rock.

"Ostrogothic" is for Pixie "Helga" Garvin Vincenz: may your other Marlene Dietrich life impart you with a little more Ostrogothic wisdom.

"Mountain River Cave" is for Li Bai, a well-known poet of the Tang Dynasty.

"Gastric Bypass," is for Ivor and Madeline White somewhere in the Balearics eating fish and chips and dodging taxes.

"The Moths and a Nymph in a Bucket of Fiery Piss," is for John Kinsella.

"A Seat at the Bar of Non-Being," is for Dr. Fortunato Vincenz, lic. iur.: may all those hours at the bar have paid off in nirvana cards. And, as for Martin Vincenz, notary public, myth-maker, little shaman facing the public prosecution, there's more to be said here: I loved those beers and the cries across the rooftops… Still, you had to go Ostrogothic.

"Once Upon a Time in Liechtenstein," is for Ray "Raycheff" Lee Davis, music producer, country music artist, HBB watch-maker, once-chain-smoker, SONY acolyte … strange, passionate man. And for Dominique Ferry Waldman, wherever and whomever they may be.

"Purge of the Apparition *(An Epilogue of Sorts)*:" two hundred billion galaxies or thereabouts. At least that's what the scientists are telling us at the moment.

"A Myth Like No Other," is for Jóhann Jóhannsson, Paul Valéry, Terry Pratchett, Alasdair Gray, Carl Sagan and Joseph Campbell. May we all meet again, on a day like this, somewhere in the far reaches of the cosmos.

"It Must Have Been Something She Ate" is for Livia (Julia Augusta) Drusilla (59 BCE–CE 29), Empress of Rome, toxicologist and evil grandmother to the Emperor Claudius (10 BCE–13 October CE 54). The epigraph originates from Robert Graves' *I, Claudius*, the screenplay.

"The Wasp Factory" is for Iain Banks or Iain M. Banks, the originator of The Culture of the Wasp: wink wink, nudge nudge (Mister Palin).

"A Very Obscure Diagnosis," is for the poet, translator, editor, teacher, intrepid fisherman, ecologist and adventurer, Mark Spitzer. RIP CE 2023. (Obscure fact: both cats and rats adore milk.)

"Into the Hands of a Holy Roman Citizen," is for my parents, Angela Margaret Seach (Vincenz), and Lorenz Vincenz Jr. (Seach)—with a brief mention of Pixie the Ostrogoth.

The Author

Marc Vincenz is a poet, fiction writer, translator, editor, musician and artist. He has published many books of poetry, fiction and translation. His more recent collections include *The Pearl Diver of Irunmani, A Splash of Cave Paint, The King of Prussia is Drunk on Stars, The Mayfly Codex,* and the novelette, *The Visitation.* His work has been published in *The Nation, Ploughshares, Raritan, Colorado Review, Washington Square*  *Review, Fourteen Hills, Willow Springs, World Literature Today, The Notre Dame Review, The Golden Handcuffs Review, The Los Angeles Review of Books* and many other journals and periodicals.

His translation of Klaus Merz' selected poems, *An Audible Blue* won the 2023 Massachusetts Book Award for Translation.

He is publisher and editor of MadHat Press and publisher of *New American Writing,* and lives on a farm in Western Massachusetts where there are more star-nosed voles, tufted grey-buckle hares and *Amoeba scintilla* than humans.

Other Books by Marc Vincenz

Poetry
The Propaganda Factory, or Speaking of Trees
Mao's Mole
Gods of a Ransacked Century
Behind the Wall at the Sugar Works
 (a verse novel)
Beautiful Rush
Additional Breathing Exercises
 (bilingual)
This Wasted Land and Its Chymical Illuminations
 (annotated by Tom Bradley)
Becoming the Sound of Bees
Sibylline
 (illustrated by Dennis Paul Williams)
The Syndicate of Water & Light
Leaning into the Infinite
Here Comes the Nightdust
Einstein Fledermaus
The Little Book of Earthly Delights
A Brief Conversation with Consciousness
 (illustrated by Sophia Santos)
There Might Be a Moon or a Dog
39 Wonders and Other Management Issues
The Pearl Diver of Irunmani
A Splash of Cave Paint
The King of Prussia is Drunk on Stars
All the Tricks of Language
IRØNCLAD
 (illustrated by Jake Quatt)
No More Animal Poems
MYTHODOLOGY
The Form of Time: New and Selected Poems

Limited Editions and Chapbooks

Benny and the Scottish Blues
    (illustrated by Darene Dewan)
Genetic Fires
Upholding Half the Sky
Pull of the Gravitons
An Alphabet of Last Rites
Thieves' Canto
The Mayfly Codex
Three Telltale Love Signs
Rocketship to the Andromeda Galaxy
Faerie Ecology
    (illustrated by Sophia Santos and Jake Quatt)

Translations

Kissing Nests by Werner Lutz
Nightshift / An Area of Shadows by Erika Burkart and Ernst Halter
A Late Recognition of the Signs by Erika Burkart
Grass Grows Inward by Andreas Neeser
Out of the Dust by Klaus Merz
Secret Letter by Erika Burkart
Lifelong Bird Migration by Jürg Amann
Unexpected Development by Klaus Merz
An Audible Blue: Selected Poems (1963—2016) by Klaus Merz
Casting a Spell in Spring by Alexander Xaver Gwerder
Country of Small Men by Ernst Halter
In the House, Still Light by Klaus Merz
Mothers Letters: Pure Caviar by Ion Monoran
    (co-translated with Marius Surleac)
Dreaming Jack by Klaus Merz

Fiction

The Visitation
Three Taos of Tao, or How to Catch a Fortuitous Elephant
City of Lemons
    (illustrated by Sophia Santos)

Graphic Novel
Coalition No. 9
    (illustrated by Jake Quatt)

Recent Titles from Unlikely Books

The Other Side of the Mirror: Excerpts and Additions to a Plantation Owner's Diary by Aileen Bassis

Dora/Lora by Larissa Shmailo

Here, Which Is Also a Place by Mark DuCharme

Handling Filth: Simple Sabotage Field Manual by Jared Schickling

White Van by Meg Tuite

Flight Advice by Tobey Hiller

A Brief Conversation with Consciousness by Marc Vincenz

~getting away with everything by Vincent A. Cellucci and Christopher Shipman

fata morgana by Joel Chace

Typescenes by Rodney A. Brown

Political AF: A Rage Collection by Tara Campbell

The Deepest Part of Dark by Anne Elezabeth Pluto

Swimming Home by Kayla Rodney

Manything by dan raphael

Citizen Relent by Jeff Weddle

The Mercy of Traffic by Wendy Taylor Carlisle

Cantos Poesia by David E. Matthews

Left Hand Dharma: New and Selected Poems by Belinda Subraman

Apocalyptics by C. Derick Varn

Pachuco Skull with Sombrero: Los Angeles, 1970 by Lawrence Welsh

Monolith by Anne McMillen

When Red Blood Cells Leak by Anne McMillen

anonymous gun. by Kurtice Kucheman

Soy solo palabras but wish to be a city with words by León De la Rosa and illustrations by Gui.ra.ga7

Blue Rooms, Black Holes, White Light by Belinda Subraman, illustrated by César Ivan

Scorpions by Joel Chace

Ghazals 1-59 and Other Poems by Sheila E. Murphy and Michelle Greenblatt

brain : storm by Michelle Greenblatt

My Hands Were Clean by Tom Bradley

ANCHOR WHAT by Vernon Frazer

www.ingramcontent.com/pod-product-compliance
Lightning Source LLC
Chambersburg PA
CBHW031420120626
46545CB00006B/2201